Gathering

June 9, 2018

*To U Mass Lowell
Honors College
on the occasion of the
Townsend Library Book Fair*

Gathering

New and Selected Poems
By MaryEllen Letarte

MaryEllen Letarte

CW Books

Published by CW Books
P.O. Box 541106
Cincinnati, OH 45254-1106

ISBN: 978-1-62549-279-1

Poetry Editor: Kevin Walzer
Business Editor: Lori Jareo

Visit us on the web at www.readcwbooks.com
Author's web site: www.maryellenletarte.com

Cover photo by the author
Author photo by James A. LaFond-Lewis

Acknowledgments

Many thanks to the editors of the following publications where a number of these poems first appeared, some in a different form or with a different title.

Lucidity Journal: "To A Friend"
Mothersalwayswrite.com: "Great Grandma on Peggotty
     Beach"
Silver Boomer Books: "Autumn Afternoon," "Apple"
Sudden Marigolds: An Anthology of poems: "The Writer"
The Bay State Echo: "Plea in Winter," "Spring Mud,"
     "Women are the Best Travelers," "War and
     Lunch"
The Mass State Poetry Society Anthology: "Spring Death," "A
     Barred Owl," "Murder at Lake Naivasha," "She
     Gardens with her Son on Her Ninety-Fifth
     Birthday," "That One Glorious Season"
The Outdoor Enthusiast: "A Barred Owl"
Verse Wisconsin: "War and Lunch," "Old Women Are the
     Best Travelers," "Woodside in Autumn," "Life in
     Death"
Troubadour21.com: "Weeds"

Thank you

To the Louise Bogan Poets for reading my poems with generous hearts. Also to Sarah Busse, Jeanette Maes, Steve Priest, and Barbara Rollins, editors and writers who were the first to include my poems in publications they edited and issued. And to the many unnamed poets who have contributed to my growth, not only as a writer, but, as a member of the human family. And to my husband, Richard, for his unfailing support and encouragement.

For My Granddaughters

Katrina Mueller, Celeste Ross, Quinlan Ross
Cecile Letarte, Sylvie Letarte

Contents

.

Things I Don't Throw Away

A gray stone cradled in the palm of my hand,
a celebration of rock-rubbing survival.

A plastic Buddha, with long earlobes and a half smile,
meditating on the window sill.

A creased copy of *Blue Estuaries* scented with laven-
der and thumbed by readers led to Louise Bogan.

A blanket covered with lilac butterflies treasured by
my children, grandchildren, and by my mother.

A hand-made card that says, *Look who's twenty-three*,
read every year for forty-nine years.

A Texas-heart fossil sitting on a cluttered ledge, be-
side photos of loved ones' loved ones.

Thread bare beret I can't bear to throw away.
I'll recycle, save the threads for tying braids.

Note to comfort me when my sister lay dying,
I lost her, yet she's here.

The taste of my husband's peanut buttered lips, and
his photo taken after he recovered from malaria.

Leaf saved from a side garden of the Taj Mahal,
lemon and mango trees growing in my dreams.

An American Girl

You were born from the mountains of Haiti,
the lavender of France, the red grapes of Italy with
dashes of Anglo kings and the dust of Welshmen
mixed in.

A sprinkle of Russian royalty and Irish scallywag adds
to your lack of pedigree and your perfection. Your
latte skin and jet black hair are warm enough for any
tribe to hallmark as their own. But I claim you.

Granddaughter darling mine, I claim you as my own
and you're mine.

War and Lunch

Lean words spread like soft cheese
and ground ham on rye.

In short gasps we laugh, the sound saves
this black May day. We are not versed for war.

Guns doffed by young and old kill
old and young. No one knows the facts.

We are not told. Kin kills kin,
some live with pork and beans.

War is sold as the way for peace.
Do we know where peace is?

We meet for lunch, head to head
strife we mix with bread, with beer.

John plays the mouth harp, we hear him
… from the hills, from the lake,

the soup grows cold.

Women are the Best Travelers

Old women move from country to country,
like tireless trams they crawl up hills, traverse
the lakes and greet each other passing by.

On the move, they keep on moving,
without a thought to hold them back
they move to rap and rat-a-tat-tat.

Old women wish old men would stay
in their own countries and play their games
without sending their children to war.

Begin Again

She writes to fill the air with poems,
doesn't slow her pen when words
jump off the page or verses shake.

Her rolling syncopated shake
flings commas & adverbs from her poems.
Nouns tap, verbs hum. Shaker-like words

endure. We feel the chorus of words
surround us with a blissful shake,
forever changing us and our poems.

When words shake into poems we begin again.

Great Grandma on Peggotty Beach

Great Grandma in her black-taffeta bathing suit
waded in the Atlantic Ocean,
before storms toppled the houses,
before sand washed into the marsh
and sent herons flying.

One summer I lived in a shore house,
struggled to swim. I wanted to wear long hair
knotted in braids. I wanted to float on the waves, like
Great Grandma and her friends.
They swam and walked the beach,
but spoke only Italian.

Buongiorno, I said.

Great Grandma and I gathered green and amber glass
and other tide treasures, lost now like her stories. I
wish I knew why she had a cross blued on her arm
and why she burned it off.

I do know she sailed into the Port of Boston in 1913
with her thin sons. They learned English,
but she didn't. She expected to die young.

May

I hold my coat closed,
shiver in the longer days,
as the fuzzy tree limbs
hail the red and green nodes.
Bushes expose their color
and robins pick up straw.

Trills, chirps, and peeps
return me to another May
when forsythia poked through
a cover of snow and cheered
my dying mother. She wanted
to stay to smell the lilacs,
to watch the fledglings.

"I'll miss you." She said.
And birds twittered as we
prayed, *Hail Mary full of grace.*

The Orange

When I peel an orange, each piece
releases the aroma of my mother and
her great granddaughter.

That day I gave one juicy section
to my mother, saved a slice for me,
presented the rest to my granddaughter,
who slurped and dripped, filled the room
with sunshine.

For one delicious moment we inhaled
the colors of the sun.

Survival

Leaves of the magnolia grow too plump. I prefer wide-leafed hostas that dare to variegate and shelter small creatures. In my garden hostas survive plummets, as hawks dive for their supper. Drama at the window! Crows arrive first and frighten a chipmunk that runs through my open doorway. I jump up, bump a Mason jar and slide to the floor along with water and sunny petals. I laugh as the chipmunk careens in the corner. He finds the way out and I find the way up.

spotted leaf patch
verdigris tints pebbles
snail shells add decor

Touch the Blue Sand of My Island

Trees wet with a dozen twilights melt in the blued haze while I write café au lattéd in my bed. You give me words through small slits in the curtain. The nouns and verbs connect to lift me over the sky where I find the sunny side of the ocean cluttered with red tape and plastic bottle caps used as hats by whales that have shrunk into seahorses. Dolphins ride the waves. They jump the nets filled with wailing tuna fighting for freedom they never knew they had. I un-knot the tangled mesh serenaded by rumbles in the kitchen. I pour a cup of coffee, drink with my eyes sanded shut, savor each roasted scent until the sun sweeps up, accompanied by the garbage truck.

The Hunger and the Gatherers

From the corner of my eye
through my picture window
a cardinal flies by
then a blue jay, jay-jays,
a chick-a-de, de-dees.
A turkey opens his beak like a shovel,
scoops seed down his gullet.
I rap on the window.
Tom turkey flaps
trots into the woods.

My father would have shot
that turkey dead,
then cleaned and cooked
the meat for turkey soup
after giving me a feather
for my collection.

Generations of Peas

I'd vowed never to force my children to eat—
Dad had sat me at the table until every pea was gone.
In napkins, in pant cuffs, and on any ledge
they disappeared.

My husband, Rich, always cleaned his plate
and ate what remained on mine. That night
he cajoled and frowned as our small son nibbled at
peas and meatloaf.

I want ice cream. I'm not hungry, our son said.

One more bite—here, take a forkful—eat up—
—no ice cream without a clean plate—eat, eat.
You won't grow tall—open up. Let's eat, my husband
said.

No! No. Our son answered.

You may leave the table, if you're finished,
I declared.

Rich continued to cajole, to threaten,
our son clamped his mouth shut
—I turned red—

Neither noticed.

I swept the plate off the table,
scarred the kitchen floor
for all to see.

Plea in Winter

February! Your grey light
hides spring under the snow.

Warm me with winter berries
and holly that peak through.

Let the sun reflect hope
for days filled with primrose.

Send all that I need
to endure this frozen earth.

Let your sun shine on icy crystals
and sparkle in a child's eyes.

On a Pond

She watched, still as a stone,
      as I skated past her small form.

The moment I called she grabbed
      my hand and we glided together
      in private formation.

—time froze, she let go—
      a smile slid—across—her pursed lips.

             She   skimmed away.

Recycling

My ashes will mix with your ashes and we'll be
    specks in morning dew.

We'll be lasting embers of the celestial divine—
    stories that rise from moon to moon.

We'll be blown through the open door to be lint
    on the bishop's robe.

We'll be compost under pines for lady-slippers,
    yours and mine.

We'll be sails for the Asian flu and food for the
    pecking hen.

We'll be mixed with clouds and rain on the
    purple beyond.

We'll be flecks in the paper maché.

We'll be dandelion seeds that wild in the
    yard, born again as light of the sky.

We'll be stars more brilliant than Rigel or Vega.

Sixth Grade Photo

There he is, a flash of himself,
sturdy in his white shirt and striped tie
unlike the others, slouched,
dark ties limp at their thin necks.

Their faces shadowed, his lit
with a smile. Girls noticed,
that year, he learned to dance.

I fell in love with him,
didn't see his ties.

He wore a uniform,
became my officer, my gentleman,
fully equipped with wit and a two-step.

**

His uniform gaps at his chest
and he dances on my toes, but he
still wows me with his wit
and his ties have not decomposed.

Fragments

She reached toward me, her cherished gift
crushed between her thumb and finger.
She dropped the cheerio in my palm,
I fell in love.

*

Her seaweed eyes lit up,
tears slid down her round cheeks.
She gave me a tissue to dry her face,
we laughed.

*

She called my name,
I'll never be the same.

Autumn Afternoon

Yesterday's leaves
hang loose, float
into moldy mulch.

Knowledge of tomorrow
hides within the limbs
of children and oaks
untroubled by clouds.

Grandmothers hover,
trees shiver,
acorns plunk.

Red is the Color of Joy

My Grandfather Meets His Wife

The handy-man, Mr. Lewis, entered the paint-chipped schoolhouse, stuffed leaky windows with cardboard scraps. He eyed the school marm, Miss Ruggles, as she directed her students. She's a natural, he said to himself. The youngest pupil squirmed, grasped a pencil, practiced printing while older students read Psalms from a black leather Bible. Others, close to graduating, sat in corners and wrote hero stories on unused newsprint-paper. Thank you, Mr. Lewis, Miss Ruggles said. You've arrived just in time to keep out the storm. The next day Mr. Lewis hummed, chopped wood and carried in logs, a chore the oldest boys relished, but not that day; Mr. Lewis did it. He wanted to say hello to the blue-eyed teacher. Miss Ruggles looked up as she glided toward her students. Mr. Lewis gave a nod, noticed her slim ankles. Good afternoon! she said. Stunning as a cardinal in a winter apple tree.

Years Later

Handyman is not an easy career. Mr. Lewis and his family moved from place to place before settling on a farm in Wisconsin. Along with six children came failing health and desperation. By then my grandfather drove the tractor, planted seed, and pulled weeds only in his memory. He sat on his gray-splintered porch, nodding to the mourning doves and to his gleeful daughter running toward mockingbirds. Grandma plowed straight rows from the high seat of the rusted tractor followed by her sons planting beets and potatoes. The boys learned to hunt as well as plant for winter eating. The jars of squirrel meat and pigeon looked gruesome lined up on cellar shelves beside the beets and potatoes. Exhausted from working morning to night, Grandma dreamed of teaching in the red schoolhouse. She prayed her daughter would have a better life.

Decades After

A red book with the worn embossed letters, *The Poems of Oliver Wendell Holmes*, arrived in the mail, a surprise from my brother wishing me a Happy Birthday. Inside the cover, a clear "Catherine Ruggles" is written. My grandmother read the Bible. I never heard her read a poem other than the Psalms; she must have cherished the Holmes volume or it would have gotten lost when she moved from home to home after leaving the failed farm. I wish I could thank her for saving the poetry book with the red cover. I'd ask her to read "Old Ironsides" and then share all those stories she began and never finished because her tears flooded them away, like the time she told me how she'd discovered her sister had died. She read it in the obituaries.

Amaryllis

Listen!
Hear the rustle,
the first leaf reaches for the sun.

The hour fades, petals fall,
they gather in the garden of time.

Under Glass

He and his fiancé described tiny figurines
too high for me to see. Later the statuettes
and netsuke they adored became dear.

He had numerous nieces and nephews,
but he took *me* to the museum. My quiet
nature, or maybe my name, the same
as his fiancé, set me apart.

The day he married I carried the guest book,
asked people to sign; it took all
my ten-year old courage.

Years later he fell behind the glass.
He asked me how I knew him.
Was I mother, sister, or friend,
he asked me how I knew him.

Winter Wars

I'm lost in dark trees. No time for princess pine. No sun for wintergreen to raise its plump arms. Its roots war with pines, strong scents—mint and pine. Birch bend heavy with frost while oak leaves ice to black limbs. Twigs fall, velvet sound when they hit the ground. Snow beards fir and fur. Protons, electrons, rise, combine, collapse, rejoin, unlink collection connection sparks not war but new direction.

no one hears the link
wintergreen plumps
bonsai for summer

Murder at Lake Naivasha

For Joan Root (1936–2006)

I adored the speedy hippos,
spitting cobras, and crocodiles
that Joan photographed
in Kenya.

She saved crippled animals,
cleaned fetid water,
and protected the land
from machete-toting marauders
and warthogs.

She loved Lake Naivasha.

The day Joan was killed I dreamed
I saw puff adders choke on their frogs,
fish eagles drop their prey,
hornbills abandon their young,
and Joan adopt a child
who married mine.
Together our children
saved Lake Naivasha.

Brides Wanted

In those days we prayed for children in China, donated our piggy-bank savings. "Save the children! Sacrifice, send your pennies." The nuns echoed the missionaries. "There's not enough food, children have nothing to eat, nowhere to sleep. Some are left by the side of the road." Sacrificing didn't help but our pennies might have. Now the Chinese don't need money for food, they need brides for the boys not left by the side of the road.

cries confetti the air
two by two in the Ark
ten thousand mums

Dear Ivy,

How's your journey? Not too tiring, I hope, as you stretch from brick to brick. My work here in the country has been soaring. The birds fly by and brush my seeds across the green. This spreading gold is marvelous. I never dreamed it would be so glorious filling the field with my offspring. If you ever want to return to your daffodil kingdom by all means invite me in. I imagine you have a similar reason to wake up every day. I do miss you in your past disguises. You were wonderful as morning glory, but as daffodil you were the best. The neighbors and certain family members would frown at our mixing, but they never liked weeds spicing their green backyards or rumbling in their beds. And you know how I adore being with you, my dear old friend. When will I see you again?

Love,
Dandelion

Irish or Not

We knew our front yard had everything—
lilacs, tiger lilies, even an old apple tree to climb.
When we searched the backyard, green and lush,
Dad helped us.
Look! A four-leaf clover.

I'm not Irish, he said.
He'd seen too many signs,
Irish Need Not Apply,
to claim shamrocks.
I am American.

To a Friend

For J. H. D.

I miss you
when I'm away.

I miss the words
that fly out of your mouth
like a cloud of starlings
        finding their home
        in the perfect tree.

I miss your smile,
brilliant, it's the sun
that floods the frozen lake
        leaves crystals
        to catch the warm rays.

I miss your laugh
excited and full
like Pooh Bear
        reaching into a hive
        and slurping a cache of honey.

I miss you when I'm away
but not tonight.
I'll stay.

Generations of Blueberries

I remember berry picking with Dad
        on the hill under the high wires,
        on the hill where bugs buzzed,
        where briars bit, where berries
        stained me blue, but didn't stop
        my skin from pinking through.

I remember that first pie-taste of blueberry,
it stopped the itchy bites and burning skin.

Is there anything sweet as wild berry pie?

My granddaughter's blueberry kiss.

Today at the farm plump berries
hang on wide bushes. Row after row,
after row. They wait for my granddaughter
to pick and plop them in her plastic pail.
She is dazzled by neon signs that blink:
        ice cream, souvenirs,
           ice cream, souvenirs.

I buy her an ice cream cone and a ball
then wonder if she will remember the farm,
the blueberries, or me.

The Pantry

She remembered a hunger so deep
her belly rattled, but I knew her
pillow-soft and dusted with flour.
We loved visiting on noodle-making-day.
Strips of dough clung on clothes racks,
the backs of chairs, on every Formica
surface. But it wasn't just the pasta,
an aroma of plum tomatoes,
onions, and fennel bubbled up
from a pot so big we could crawl into it
when it stood empty in the pantry.

And the pantry!
It was more a room than a closet.

Shelves hugged the walls
from floor to ceiling, not only overflowing
with ziti and penne, but with potatoes,
carrots, graham crackers, amoretti,
green-cork-stopped-bottles, and brown paper
sacks filled with sugar, almonds,
pistachios, anise seeds and cinnamon sticks
scattering the scent of abundance
with every swing of the door.

Weeds

In the beginning they wander
scatter seeds where they go.

They wave from the sidewalk near buttercups glow,
shake ragweed and bellwort across the old paths, feed
beetles and moths, leave lace in the grass. They creep
in the garden with lilacs and moles.

What does it matter,
nettles or rose.

Arriving

They leaned together,
touched for a moment,
on the bicycle built for two.

He didn't see her silver hair,
still auburn in his eyes.
She didn't see his wrinkled skin
only heard his melody.

Their ride through the decades
lasted till the bike collapsed
in the backyard.

Fifty years wheeling,
his swagger softened
her smile deepened.
They stepped into the house
didn't need another ride.

Talking to Summer

Flooded with poppies too many
with blossoms too red, too lush,
I reach for a wrinkled bandanna
to catch the erupting gush.

Like a rabbit chased by a fox,
I blink with a summer sneeze
and see in my teary blues
the green of a thousand trees.

I run on the outdoor path
squish go my new white Keds
too late, I've stepped on a poop
my neighbor forgot to scoop.

The gnats and giant mosquitoes
bleed me with every bite. Will
dragonflies come to my rescue
their diaphanous wings in flight?

Poppies, cowpats, and bug bites
kick up a loud disturbance
but never as bad as the sleet
or the roar of a plow on the street.

One Hundred Years

I sang senseless ballads to my infants. They liked my
croaking voice until they heard their dad sing *Edel-
weiss*. Today I hear the beats and strums of grandchil-
dren and dance their happy songs, skipping, not sing-
ing. Toy-box trains, blue moons, dog tales, and pink
baboons riddled the children's poems to win blue rib-
bons. I'll write for years, up to the century mark like
Stanley Kunitz did, then I'll need one hundred after
that to match his mulching layers.

sailing clouds now
plum sky covers muddy street
sage with lost petals

New Flute

I drive her to her lessons then listen to her flute vibrate from the glass studio. I don't know if she practices at home, but she smiles at my house when she picks up her silver instrument. I like the toot that comes out of your flute, I tell her. Not toots, no toots, she says. How about a flue from a flute and a trum from a trumpet? Wouldn't that be fun? No, she says. Later she accompanies her cousins who play on a portable melodeon, legs and fingers pumping. We are playing the pianofluté, she says.

passion runs wild
green red orange in the trees
wren sings a love song

Empty Pews

I grieve for my youth, not for the Church.
Altar server and priesthood were closed
to girls. No chance to choose.
Maybe I would have accepted church vows
instead of traveling with children.

My holy orders became talks to myself
as I plowed into the winter of my life.
Today snow keeps me home, where I read
words of St. Francis Assisi and Agatha Christie,
then make snow angels with my grandchildren.

Christmas

You are Midnight Mass,
snow tires, and church bells,
twinkle lights, gingerbread
and peppermint candy.

You are children and grandparents
pink cheeked and giggly
sipping eggnog and hot-chocolate.

You are lighted steeples
and carolers singing Holy Night
beside Salvation Army bells.

You are shivering elves and exhausted
shoppers like the Three Kings
bowing with precious gifts
and the shepherds kneeling to the Child.

Apple

I
My granddaughter walked around
the pink granite stone—touched
the imbedded wedding photo of
Grammy and Gramps.
Where are the windows? She asked.

In my mind, I answered.
Then I told her a story about Gramps.
Tell me more. I don't have windows. She said.

II
You were the smart one
running from danger, Dad said.
It was his last blessing in the ICU
before a tube pressed in his throat
heaved air into his scarred lungs.
That day I stayed afraid. I didn't run.
I heard the last hiss of the blue tube,
saw Dad's life pass away,
like a thousand monarchs
ascending from an old apple tree.

III
Years later my granddaughter climbed
a backyard tree, crowded with a hundred apples.
She picked the fruit, shook the limb, then said.
*Let's make pie, I'll peel, Pep can cut; will you
make the crust and add a story?*

Out of Focus

The grandfather I never met
went from pioneer to poor farmer
in a short lifetime.

His unripe sons, including Dad,
flew east to serve their country—
returned as men who embraced
city life and modern women.

Dad became a plastics pioneer,
chemistry his hoe for recycling
toys and dishes. He ground down,
melted, dyed, and re-molded
before it was the-thing-to-do.

I learned to sow what I needed:
books, maps and unexpected
highways, and house plants.

My children keep herb gardens,
return home to hear old stories
of their grand-dad and his dad hoeing.

Brave 1959

Grass clawed at my plaid slacks,
mosquitoes hummed, gnats bit.
My brother and his friend kicked
up hay and insects with their Keds.
I looked for stray cows.

A tunnel appeared on the next rise.
We strained to see—saw ridges of tin.
Don't go in, I said in a whisper.
The boys stood still then bent over
and dipped in the dark.

What would I say to Mom,
what would I do if they didn't come out?

Finally, I saw the boys wave
from over the hill, at the tube's
end. They slogged home
with splotched shirts, a strange scent
and a squish as they walked.

Do it or die was their refrain.

Some boys don't tell their story.
They drown swimming across the pond,
motorcycling down Main Street,
or tunneling through the latest war.

First Day

What is that cry, do you need milk?
Soothing you is like petting a squirrel.

Precious one, you mesmerize.
My life has ceased, nothing except you,
fierce chickadee, petite wolf.

Dearest, darling girl
how will you grow into the universe?
Will I be released when palaces
open their doors for you?

Your perfection stuns,
I've slipped into the black of your eyes.

Silence in the Forest

It's the law they say. In doctors' offices and dental clinics, it's forbidden to turn off the radio when it protects private conversations. I've turned on mute to end the dings and pings on my computer and I refuse to listen to the serenades in telephones. If the tra-la-la that surrounds us would whisper like the trees, I'd whisper too. Waiting in line could be serene. Maybe. Quiet space is not an option and I'm not ready for the silent place.

wrens sing for those who listen

The Writer

He would have adored haiku,
jotting three lines on life's lessons
taking the last line from his weedy garden.

Villanelle would be a problem.
He'd compare it to a dog that grabs its tail,
not much discovery though lots of action.

Monologues would be his forte. They fit
his aptitude for writing letters as vehicles
for his opinions.

Sestinas would have been his favorite,
long enough for a good story with gated edges
to keep the woodchucks out or in.

His free verse would be too terse
or maybe not, look at the *Gettysburg
Address*, brief notes on brown paper.

His sequence poems would be past and present
though future would be blank. His life was not
what he expected.

They Went Home

I miss the grandchildren, the blue sky, and sunshine.
The spring has not opened its eyes. I want to see the
peach fuzz on the trees and gold on the bushes. I
want to feel the sun on my face and in my house. I
want to rejoice in quietness, to hear titmice and spar-
rows chirp along with the nuthatch. They do not fly
when I approach; they see that I'm the one who seeds
the feeder. The roads are treacherous with winter
heaves. I'm in the annex of my children's lives. I walk
to wake up the poems locked in my cupboard.

purple sky silence
crows caw at mulching fields
the empty window

Contentment

I found you in the swish of the trees
    in the pebble-lined stream
    in the scratch of a pen
    in the tap of a key.
I found you in the dark of the ocean
    in the light-spray of stars
    in late summer asters and
    in one chocolate kiss.
Running in the street
    in the rustle of satin
    in the hands of my lover, I found you.
I found you in the gold of smooth marble
    and in knot of the wood.
In attic and basement I found you,
    in purple of sweet lavender
    in lilac growing wild
    under the rocks and in the garden,
    everywhere I found you.

Where are you now?

Thoughts After Viewing "My Studio," by Eleanor Norcross

A music score leans on a piano, and
I imagine myself practicing *Rhapsody in Blue*.

Staring at the pattern of the studio carpet
I slip back sixty years, play marbles
on our Persian rug. Dad is young
and smiling not like Eleanor's father,
with gray beard and slipper-shod feet.

It would have been lovely if Dad
had taught me piano or encouraged
music lessons. Easy Listening was his choice
when he sat clad in overworked boots
and plaid shirt penciling a puzzle in the paper.
He told me he dreamed of playing piano.
Now when my grandchildren play
I see Dad in his recliner, listening.

My Father Taught Me

Rounding the corner, I heard what sounded like crickets and tiny ting-a lings. Then I saw them, children riding tricycles with bells on their handlebars. They circled in an empty tennis court. A six-foot man encouraged the children, *good job, stay straight, feel the wind,* as they rode around the net. The children stopped and looked when the man left the court to get water from his van. The moment he returned they resumed pedaling. I never had a tricycle but I did get a bike on my tenth birthday, which I crashed racing down a hill that same day. No help from my dad then, he drove tractors not bicycles. My balance was bad and unfortunately has not changed since then, but let's skip that and go right to where my father was able to help me like that father helped his bicycling tots. It was in first grade. I believed books held secrets but I couldn't read. My father worked with me one letter at a time. The words looked too complicated to ever understand, but they snapped into focus and I read on and on.

awakening
dandelions, sunflowers
golden summer field

Celestial

She's like bread that rises
leaving a balm in the air.
I'm cinnamon with a touch of cayenne
and lemon essence. I'm nutmeg.
She's my strawberry-muffin.
Much too soon she'll be mixing the batter,
making her own sweet pastry.

Morning Entertainment

Swallows stream in iridescence,
a swash of purple for the dawn
not a dee from chickadees or
whir and whine from blue jays.
I start the day tossing bird seed
and pouring children's cereal.

Squirrels gnaw holes in feeders,
tumble like star acrobats,
and stuff their cheeks, like clowns.
I fertilize the plants then toss
more seed to watch the show.

Ants pick up crumbs from
fresh baked bread, suck juice
from ripe plums. Back porch
marauding is okay, the cellar too,
but not where I bake sweet-bread
to sell at harvest fairs along
with cheese bread, the one
the ants like to tunnel through.

Deer bump the garden's fence
nibble at stalks and green buds.
I see them from the kitchen window
as I munch chocolate bars and gummy
bears taken from the children's stash.

Turkeys mosey around the compost pile.
If I walk too close, they cluck and flap.
A frightened turkey could knock me down,
you'd think they know I roast their cousins
each Thanksgiving Day.

Lavender Sea

The color startled me down the path.
I walked toward the vision
      saw the pink sky mix with the sea.

Not purple like a starfish from the Pacific
or the violet of a sea anemone
      but lilac like the earliest May blossom.

The color ebbed and flowed until noon
when the ocean turned midnight blue
      as clouds shuttled through.

Each May I look for the lilac sea,
find it blooming by my back-door.

Christmas Gift

She read poetry daily,
loved to get pulled into a novel.

After much consideration,
he bought and wrapped,
set the red-bowed package
under the tinseled fir tree.

She opened it, laughed.

Books tumbled out,
their doubles back to back
on her bookshelf.

A Starling (or is he a sibling?)

crashes into my dreams.
He blinks his eyes, flaps his wings
        stretches over the black pavement.

When shadows lengthen, he whistles in whisper.

Then inching near a yew shelter, he flops his way under the bush until black mulch (chocolate pudding?) swallows him whole.

Then I fly into the starless night far from the brambles of sated starlings, squash soup, and iPhone marauders.

New World Soliloquy

Chickadee, blue-jay, titmouse
      take turns   fly
          in and out
             at the window feeder.

Falcon
      Skylark
Firebird
        driven in rhythm
        merge on the Jersey Pike.

Instinct and gears shift away from aggression.

Morning Reunion

I answer your moan,
ignore the dove's call on the wind.

You are the wind that climbs the eaves,
you mix with the sun.

I welcome another day.

Dragonfly

Her days of eating moths
and flies are short unlike the years
she swam in Mirror Lake
and lived on reedy things.

She flits in green apparel
waves among the reeds,
a mate appears, grasps,
ensures dragonflies
survive another year.

In the tangle of weeds and wind
I remember when I could fly
to distant shores and test my wings.

Daily Voyage

Without a switch
I'm like a sundial—
slow and steady.

I'm a rose who can't hold its bloom,
a sun that climbs and steps down,
a yo-yo in motion.

Sleep is my journey
too soon interrupted
by two o'clock horizons.

I lose the shore of my comfort,
sail on the sapphire waves
found in early morning hours.

Epithalamion for Grandparents

She swung in a hammock
on a steamer to somewhere,
landed with teeming masses.

He arrived as a young man,
found his way as a stone cutter,
moved to suburbs with his bride.

Their home a cozy nest
amid a Victorian cluster
of scurry and clutter.

She cooked long noodles,
hung clothes, wiped cheeks.
He cleared brush, grew grapes,
made wine.

Memories of vines now lie
in a graveyard with roses
and ivy intertwined.

Photos fascinate great-great
grandchildren who never tasted
her ravioli or his red wine.

Their house still stands,
its pointy roof and colored trim,
a relic of other days
now layered in time.

Wisdom

Dad left me with snippets of truth.
I'll be fertilizer, he often remarked.
Life isn't what you expect, was another.
Sometimes he'd say, I wish I had known.
Known what?
He'd repeat, I wish I had known.
His wisdom hovers on the wind
when I walk in the woods. To feel
him near I lean on his walking-stick
carved from an old oak limb.

St. Christopher

We prayed to God, to Jesus, to Mother Mary, to the Holy Spirit (female, of course), to St Jude, St. Martha, St Mary, St. Elizabeth, especially to St. Elizabeth (my mother's name.) I don't remember ever praying to St. Robert, is there a St. Robert? Robert, my father, wasn't a saint but he had a sharp mind on wide shoulders. We prayed to St. Christopher, St. Nicholas, St. Catherine, St. Margaret. The Church told us to. It's what we did in need, in joy, in sorrow, in laughter, in tears. In all our work, in all our play, in all our trouble we prayed. It gave us time to think. Time passed, I lived without the saints as the Church rejected old stalwarts like St. Christopher. Soon half the Catholic churches of Fitchburg shuttered their steeples: St. Bernard's, Immaculate Conception, Sacred Heart of Jesus, and the Madonna of the Holy Rosary. But as always, through lost litanies, I find solutions for broken hearts, broken toys, and unresolved disagreements.

seedlings survive
transcendental meditation
the altar is bare

Reading on the Hill

The boy had his head down
he didn't see dragon clouds or the man
riding a horse brandishing a gun,
a flag trailing in the mist.

He sat still on a grassy mound.
I read *Fairy Tales* under the
oak tree, no acorns bounced
there wasn't a sound.

I looked up,
a cloud transformed
to a billowy princess
who hid her peas in the wind,
not one went in her mouth
or under her mattress.

Wizards rose from my book.
I strolled to the hillock,
Pegasus followed.

And still I read while
tears wet my cheeks and
the boy sleeps.

Postcard from the Beach

I'm three minutes from my condo
with its breakfast nook big enough
for two to read the newspaper, sip coffee
and comment on the perfect weather.
After jam and bread, I'll return to the open
light of my studio facing the duck pond
where coot and teal swim without a fuss,
unlike us. I miss you.
Come!

Wedding Dress

Inspired by a Photograph

Azure, Mom's younger sister,
didn't wear the dress I found
in my Gran's hope-chest.
A sky-blue ribbon that matched
the color of Auntie's eyes,
trimmed the dress.

When Auntie was born Mom wanted
to call her Bleu. Gran said Azure
leaves no bitter aftertaste.

These three women carried me through.
Gran read nursery rhymes, Mom taught
me how to plow a field. I learned to keep
the harrow straight when I was thirteen.
Then Auntie brought me downtown.

Auntie sent letters from London
and San Francisco, not sorry
she never wore that wedding dress.
I didn't dream of Prince Charming
or farming, she said.

Mom wore that dress when she married.
There was no money for satin and long veils.
I'll wear it tomorrow—something old,
something blue.

I wish Gran were here to see me
walk down the aisle. She'd like my man—
a farmer who reads poetry, like she did.

Night and Day

A sunflower turns away
its head bent with the twilight
like an old lady, her back curved
from dreams not lived.

The sky pinks
the morning-glory opens
the baby's hand uncurls
grasps her new world.

Spring

Liz and her dog
      plodding along,
      iris, jonquils
      sleep by the path,
Liz and her dog
      quicken their pace,
      hyacinth blooms
      look at the sky,
Liz and her dog
      dance in the yard,
      sniff the fresh air,
      laugh at the mice,
Liz and her dog
      hear the birds mate
      in the fruit trees
      a nest full of straw
Liz and her dog
      attacked by the ants
      prance up and down
      shake out the pests
Liz and her dog
      stung by who-knows
      run to and fro
      jump in the pond
Liz and her dog
collapse in a heap.

Magnolia Leaf

Unbearable sun pales
veined green plumpness

to a bronze ribbon
twisting from its source.

Then weightless
edges catch the air.

It floats to the
windowsill
waving to
the earth,

shrinking,
shrinking,
shrinking
into dust.

Daffodil to a Dandelion

You are brilliant, you cannot be a weed.

Oh, but I am. Let's dance in the air,
and play on the earth.

I cannot, this bed is my life.

He withered away,
she scattered her brilliance.

That One Glorious Season

My husband's paper route started it all,
a notice at the newsstand read, *Raise
Money for Jimmy Fund, Meet Ted Williams.*

He stood in front of hardware stores and
people's banks, asked friends and family
to fund great cures.

"I won, I won," says Richie, shaking Ted's hand
in the dugout. Both smile at the camera.
He meets Billy and Mel too, and Jackie Jensen looks
him in the eye. "Stay in school, Richie,
that's more important than baseball."

He shares his baseball-stories with friends and old
Navy pals. Our children see him with Ted
in a photo album. "Way to go, Dad," they say.

He interviews Dusty Rhodes and Bob Shaw.
One page at a time he jots the stats.
Dusty calls. "Get the book done, Richie,
we ain't getting any younger, ya know."

Evenings, Sundays, and holidays
he writes of Newcomb, Garver, Shantz,
and those who had one great year.

He lives with pennant winners and batting champs,
Cy Youngs and MVP's. They all come together in,
That One Glorious Season.

Our grandchildren smile from the back cover—
as if they knew that time when baseball ruled the
sporting world.

To Marie, Living in Asia

In 1968, I found a place to build a home,
prepared for you, dear daughter, first born.
The backyard was an Eden though snakes lurked
near the jade trees and birds-of-paradise.

The glamour of being married to a Naval
officer shipped out with the Mauna Kea,
known by the wives, as the USS Forever Sail.
It steamed to the Tonkin Bay to supply the
Pacific Fleet with bombs and boys.

You burst into life too soon, or was the ship just too
late? Your Dad sent tapes, "Welcome to the world,
Marie. I'll be home soon." When he stepped on
shore, you knew his voice.

Now you are drawn to the East to see those places
that your father knew. It's something
you want to do.

I linger at the airport-security-gate. You fly away to
create a world that's your own. Please write about the
orchids that bloom at your door.

I see oak leaves, brown and rust in my yard,
dream of jade and bird-of-paradise.

A Tritina for Q

Fiddleheads lie asleep, ferns
closed tight. They spring open
with the warm rain. Quin's fingers,

soft, perfect, chubby fingers
dance like the potted ferns.
Hands, eyes, limbs, reach open

delicate and wild, all relax open.
Unrestrained! Sprouts lift their fingers,
light green they welcome spring. A fern

for Quin. Fern and fingers open to the sun.

With her Son on her Ninetieth Birthday

She cannot recall what she's begun,
like a bloom that flares in light
then folds at night, yet she names
the blossoms: tulips, dahlias, iris,
that glorify her yard.

She asks for tools to dig the dirt
then nods and waits for him to help.
He guides her hoe and she delights
in bulbs, in roots, and his firm hand.

Spring Mud

There is no death in snow,
light crystals hide its darkness.

Death appears in spring mud.

It doesn't leave until iris
speak to the sun.

Lost Arts

She learned ingenuity at fashion school,
took frayed trousers and stained blouses,
snipped quilt squares and tore undershirts
to make long strips for tomato garden ties.

She cut buttons from worn clothes,
popped red, brown, and white
into an old cake tin for another day.

Her great granddaughters love to eat
tomatoes off the vine, to play with buttons,
and to hear stories from Grammy's time.

Spring Death 2008

She looked out at the new snow,
thought of the long dark cold.
Sadness filled her like a spring

flooding the fields. She knew that spring
would come, melt the tired snow
with or without her. She didn't like the cold,

but she saw the daffodils flourish in the cold.
There would be long life for the buds of spring,
but not for her. She cried with the melting snow.

The snow melted into darkness that cold spring.

The Music of Tritinas

My window faces the whispering trees
that move with grace even after the wind
furies the green and all the leaves shiver,

tatter and tear. A convulsive shiver
snaps the acorns and sprigs from the trees;
they tap on the roof and eaves as the wind

wraps the house in song. Then the wind
turns until the shutters sway and shiver
and music spills from my pine and oak trees.

The trees and I shiver with the wind.

I planted the pine and oak woods
to wander in; then planted reeds
among the trees to form a path

for dragon flies. The shaded path
meanders through the woods
to meet a stream rippled with reeds.

Folded damselflies rest on the reeds
while squirrels gnaw acorns on the path.
Jay-jay-jay calls me to the woods.

Woods, path, and reeds dance to streamside.

Come! Rejoice with me when music
glides over the sylvan. This place,
with its gift of trees, comforts whether

I'm at the windowpane or in the weather.
The fir, oaks, and maple replenish my music,
create harmony in the brook. My place

by the stream shimmers. It is the place
of dreams in calm or stormy weather.
I quiet and listen to the flow of music.

Music echoes from this place in all weather.

Wrack

Mockingbirds mimic the bray
of a mule, a kitten's peep.
Those white-patched birds can
imitate fifty-four songs an hour.
Pelicans catch fish and debris,
create slurries for the nursery.
Power lies in the pouch, apple-red
when she's ready for her young.
She claps her beak, calls her partner
to fish. When plastic bags trap their feet
or hooks pierce their beaks they groan
and the mimics imitate.

They Say Climbing

Fuji
can be wild.
Unexpected risks
and dangers lie ahead
like a long marriage, easy
to begin hopeful, difficult to
sustain later. Step straight ahead,
beware of steep treks, rocky layers, blind
spots. Years heaped onto cracked highways
block the path to true endearment until
laughter arcs from cold mist, blurs
cliffs, crags and fissures, sends
a wide beacon to meadows
and distant hills. It shines
on troubled hikers to
soothe them
home.

Light Beyond the Lighthouse

For Ida Lewis (1842-1911)

Ida looked out the lighthouse window
saw one boy climb a tall mast
then the catboat rocked over.

Four struggled to stay afloat. Ida rowed out,
hauled the boys onto her small boat.
That year, 1858, was the first of many
daring rescues. She was sixteen.

At sixteen I swam in the ocean,
danced at every wedding
and kissed a wavy-haired boy
at Sand Hills Lighthouse.

Ida received a dozen marriage
proposals and had a waltz named after her
but she left her chosen spouse
to light the lanterns, to polish the lens
and rescue swamped sailors.

I never rescued anyone
but waltzed into forty-five years
of marriage. Three children
and five granddaughters followed.

Not brave, I adore the wild surf
while standing beside my husband
looking out a beach house window.

A Visit from a Barred Owl

He blinked, black eyes wide,
as I neared the fir wood.

His spotted ascot and striped vest
reminded me of an Uncle who sat by the fire
until embers grew cold in the hearth.

His head turned, I walked past,
he not perturbed by my move.
I feared he'd be gone on my return,
but found him still as before.

My old camera clicked and clacked,
he did not stir, I inched closer,
he raised his wings, I stepped back.
He stared, claws fixed on the limb.

A Prayer

Let me delight in summer
to renew my spirit.
as green echoes the trees
and months cycle into
a thousand hues of ripeness.

You are my garden.

Let me greet the fall
to renew my spirit as
days turn rich with russets
and the sculptured orchard
bestows her red beauties.

You are my strength.

Let me invite the winter
to renew my spirit as
gray paints the earth,
leaves space for crystals
to kiss the land white.

You are my laughter.

Let me rejoice in spring
to renew my spirit as
crocus open and cover
the earth with rainbow glee
while grandchildren dance
my world new.

Winter's Green

Juniper and princess pine
inch across the darkened woods
add emerald bursts to forest floor
and spiciness to gusty wind.

Wintergreen under snow and
twigs, alive in every season,
crawls along the battered ground
sending glossy dapples.
Fragrance scatters with a nudge
and flowers bob and twist
while leaves in autumn purple-red
bunch with berries sweet
edibles for you and me.

Life in Death

She was a tree,
       leaves, amber, bone, and rust
tall and short limbs
       a flutter in the air
elbows and cheeks
       rough bark and smooth
hair long, tied in back
       knots in the wood
sad melodies trailing.

She stays with us,
            a whistle, the wind,
            time shared, a song.

Personals

The moon intrigues me but I'm not ready for rocket speed. Travel gives me a headache unless I'm going south in winter. Space travel could be hell into eternity. Plus if I don't eat enough fresh orange and green things, I turn gray. I saw a coot once at Juno Beach, he had green feet and an orange spot on his beak and another above his back-bent knee. I wonder if it would retain its color if it were baked and presented, "Coot Under Glass," I'd hire a cook if I could. My meals are one item grilled or flaked and the rest piled grassy on my plate. The last job I held was begging from those who live life gathering heaps of money. They give incidentals, not enough according to the non-profit's accountants. My sleep is disturbed by dreams where I pass a hat at a great party, enough is collected to buy a Monet. I'm a museum, aging without all its acquisitions. My memories are gathered in late night poetry, if forgotten I fabricate.

Woodside in Autumn

acorns
      plunk to the ground
                asters
                        sway in the woods
                                grass
                      fades under foot
                twigs
         litter the path
    ivy
twists

paper
      yellows

doors close, women sigh, men sleep,
cold grizzles the air.

MaryEllen Letarte, leader of the Louise Bogan Poets, lives in Lunenburg, Massachusetts, a rural community in central New England. She has received numerous poetry awards from the Massachusetts State Poetry Society and launched her first book of poetry, *Meandering*, a CW imprint book, in 2017. After retiring from fundraising at a regional museum she turned to writing as a way to share her thoughts and experiences with her children and grandchildren. Her poetry has been published in various online and print journals, such as *Pitkin Review*, *Verse Wisconsin*, mothersalwayswrite.com, and *Silver Boomer Books*.

96605434R00062

Made in the USA
Columbia, SC
31 May 2018